Hotshots: Mini-Stars of the Bible

Stories of famous kids in the Bible

This book belongs to ....

I am ....(Age)

People sometimes call me .... (My Nickname)

I live at ....
....

For Parents

Have you ever tried to describe your own childhood to your children?

You probably tell them of the days before the internet, four wheel drive cars, SEGA Computer games – even felt-tipped pens and you are greeted with blank faces or giggles of amusement!

It is much more difficult to help children imagine the days of the Bible, yet how important it is to help our twenty-first century families become acquainted with its people and stories. As we read these Bible adventures we see the way God has made contact with people down the years. We see his justice and tenderness, his care and trustworthiness, his power and authority. And this gives us fresh heart to believe what he says and depend on this love.

This book is designed to help children enjoy reading the Bible. The **Hotshots** series has been creatively and carefully planned as an introduction to some of the characters and themes of the Bible. It is pitched at the child's level of understanding and enjoyment, to show how the ageless Book relates to the child's world of the here and now.

There are 60 sections covering some narratives from the Old and New Testaments. The Bible passages are included so the children can access them easily. The version is the Bible Society's *Contemporary English Version* – widely recommended for children and adults alike.

It is our prayer that through this book, the children will begin to love the Bible and become familiar with it. We also hope that it will help them to know that God is near, that he welcomes them and that they can trust him.

Getting Started with Hotshots

The Bible is a very old book. It is also a very large book. Where do you start?

You can read the Bible with the Hotshots! They are a fun group – and they are learning heaps about God and the Bible.

Choose a time and place to do your Hotshots reading.

What you will need:
- A pen
- Scissors
- Coloured pencils or pens
- Put the important things you discover in a scrapbook or on a computer.

On the clock draw the time when you will read Hotshots.

In the frame draw the place.

Meet the HOTSHOTS

They're a Sensation!

You are invited to read the Bible with Jeff and the Hotshots team. Draw yourself with the team and put your name on the extra player card.

You can listen in, sharpen your skills and have fun with them as they practise with their leader, Jeff, who helps them discover great things about the Bible and life as well as basketball.

They love their times with Jeff and we hope you do too. He's a great friend – and the tallest guy they've ever seen!

The Hotshots read the Bible …

The Bible helps them meet God and they are interested to learn that they're not the first kids to do that. In fact there's lots of kids in the Bible. We've called them **'Mini-stars'** because although they may not be as tall or as smart as Jeff they sure did star for God. Jeff is teaching the Hotshots to be stars. You can join in too.

This book will guide you. In case you don't have a Bible of your own, the parts you'll need are printed in this book. There are also some Hotshot puzzles and things to think about.

The Bible bits in this book come from different parts of the Bible, both Old and New Testaments. (You'll see that kids have starred for God all through history!) We use a reference to find our way around the different parts in the Bible – it's like a street address and tells you where to look.

The first Bible bits are from Luke. Look on the Contents page of the Bible to find Luke. (It's the third book in the New Testament part of the Bible.)

Got the page? Then look down until you see the small 5 which means you've found verse 5. Now you're ready to begin.

Kids are special

Read Luke 1:5-14

⁵ When Herod was king of Judea, there was a priest by the name of Zechariah from the priestly group of Abijah. His wife Elizabeth was from the family of Aaron. ⁶ Both of them were good people and pleased the Lord God by obeying all that he had commanded. ⁷ But they had no children. Elizabeth couldn't have any, and both Zechariah and Elizabeth were already old.

⁸ One day Zechariah's group of priests were on duty, and he was serving God as a priest. ⁹ According to the custom of the priests, he had been chosen to go into the Lord's temple that day and to burn incense, ¹⁰ while the people stood outside praying.

¹¹ All at once an angel from the Lord appeared to Zechariah at the right side of the altar. ¹² Zechariah was confused and afraid when he saw the angel. ¹³ But the angel told him:

"Don't be afraid, Zechariah! God has heard your prayers. Your wife Elizabeth will have a son, and you must name him John. ¹⁴ His birth will make you very happy, and many people will be glad."

In the boxes write the names of the two old people who loved and obeyed God.

☐☐☐☐☐☐☐☐☐

was a priest

☐☐☐☐☐☐☐☐☐

was his wife

God knew all about their baby even before he was born. He had plans for him.

Colour the shapes with a dot to find the name God chose for the baby.

God knew about you too before anyone else did. He loved you before you were born. Read about it in Psalm 139:16:

> "… *with your own eyes you saw my body being formed. Even before I was born, you had written in your book everything I would do.*"

Jeff has taught the Hotshots that God always hears what they say. Now they often talk to God. You might like to pray to God too. Here's a prayer to read. While you're talking to God, add any other things you want to tell him.

Prayer: *Lord God, you're amazing the way you know all about me. Please help me to be my best for you.*

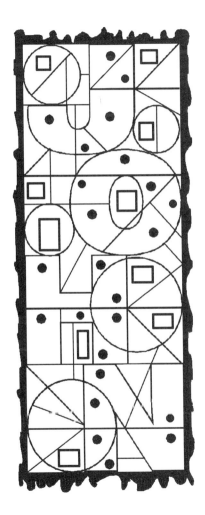

God at work

Every new baby is wonderful, but God would be with baby John in a special way. Read what the angel told his Dad.

Read Luke 1:15-17

15 "Your son will be a great servant of the Lord. He must never drink wine or beer, and the power of the Holy Spirit will be with him from the time he is born.

16 John will lead many people in Israel to turn back to the Lord their God. 17 He will go ahead of the Lord with the same power and spirit that Elijah had. And because of John, parents will be more thoughtful of their children. And people who now disobey God will begin to think as they ought to. That is how John will get people ready for the Lord."

What would John's job be?

To get people to turn back to God.

(A mirror might help you to work it out.)

Read Luke 1:18-25

[18] Zechariah said to the angel, "How will I know this is going to happen? My wife and I are both very old."

[19] The angel answered, "I am Gabriel, God's servant, and I was sent to tell you this good news. [20] You haven't believed what I've said. So you won't be able to say a thing until all this happens. But everything will take place when it is supposed to."

[21] The crowd was waiting for Zechariah and kept wondering why he was staying so long in the temple. [22] When he did come out, he couldn't speak, and they knew he had seen a vision. He motioned to them with his hands, but didn't say anything.

[23] When Zechariah's time of service in the temple was over, he went home. [24] Soon after that, his wife was expecting a baby, and for five months she didn't leave the house. She said to herself, [25] "What the Lord has done for me will keep people from looking down on me."

First Zechariah couldn't believe the angel. Then he couldn't do something else. What was it?

☐ think ☐ walk ☐ write ☐ talk

'Coach,' Emily said quietly, 'the others think I miss balls because I'm not tall enough. I should give up.'

'Stop worrying,' said Jeff. 'Remember Elizabeth in the Bible? She worried about what people were saying but God did something wonderful for her. Let's ask God to help you too.' 'Lord, Emily's worried about what the others are saying. Help her to know she's OK and that you're working in her to make her even better.'

Prayer Idea: *Do you worry about what others think about you? Talk to God about it now.*

3 Nothing is impossible

Jeff had a 'pretend' idea. 'Wouldn't it be great if we had an angel on our team. They seem to know everything before it happens! We'd win every time!'

Read about the Angel Gabriel.

Read Luke 1:26-33

[26] One month later God sent the angel Gabriel to the town of Nazareth in Galilee [27] with a message for a virgin named Mary. She was engaged to Joseph from the family of King David. [28] The angel greeted Mary and said, "You are truly blessed! The Lord is with you."

[29] Mary was confused by the angel's words and wondered what they meant. [30] Then the angel told Mary, "Don't be afraid! God is pleased with you, [31] and you will have a son. His name will be Jesus. [32] He will be great and will be called the Son of God Most High. The Lord God will make him king, as his ancestor David was. [33] He will rule the people of Israel forever, and his kingdom will never end."

Another baby! What would be special about Mary's baby?

He would be

- the S__ __ of __ __ d
- a __ __ ng f__ r __ ver

Kings die just like everyone else. Can a king last forever? Sounds impossible.

Luke 1:37 tells us something amazing – 'Nothing is impossible for God.' Write it on a card and decorate it so you can use it as a bookmark.

Prayer: *Dear God, thank you that you can do things that we think are impossible. Please remind me of that when I need it.*

Cousins

'My cousins from the country are coming to our next game.' Chris was very excited.

Do you love visiting your relations? When you meet what happens? Hugs and kisses all round? High fives? Quiet smiles?

Find out about Mary's visit to her elderly relatives, Zechariah and Elizabeth.

Read Luke 1:39-45

39 A short time later Mary hurried to a town in the hill country of Judea. 40 She went into Zechariah's home, where she greeted Elizabeth. 41 When Elizabeth heard Mary's greeting, her baby moved inside her. The Holy Spirit came upon Elizabeth. 42 Then in a loud voice she said to Mary:

"God has blessed you more than any other woman! He has also blessed the child you will have. 43 Why should the mother of my Lord come to me? 44 As soon as I heard your greeting, my baby became happy and moved inside me. 45 The Lord has blessed you because you believed that he will keep his promise."

When Mary said 'hello', what did Elizabeth say?

☐ 'Come in Mary dear, I'll get you a drink.'
☐ 'Haven't you grown since I saw you last!'
☐ 'Want to go shopping at the market?'
☐ 'God has blessed you greatly.'

Tick the right one.

Elizabeth knew Mary's baby was 'The Lord' even though he wasn't born yet!

Prayer: *Thank you Lord for all your blessings. Especially for _____ and _____.*

5 Do what God wants

The Hotshots like their team name and hope it scares the opposition!
What does your name mean?
Here are meanings of some names:

Chris – belonging to Christ   *Kim – chief*   *Emily – hard worker*
John – God's gift   *Julian – young*   *Isaac – laughter*

Ask your parents why they chose your name.

Read Luke 1:57-60

⁵⁷ When Elizabeth's son was born, ⁵⁸ her neighbors and relatives heard how kind the Lord had been to her, and they too were glad.
⁵⁹ Eight days later they did for the child what the Law of Moses commands. They were going to name him Zechariah, after his father.
⁶⁰ But Elizabeth said, "No! His name is John."

In Israel, babies used to be named after their father or someone in the family. What would people expect Elizabeth and Zechariah's baby to be called?

☐☐☐☐☐☐☐☐☐

What did they call him? ☐☐☐☐

Whose idea was that? God's!

'It's important to do what God wants, not just what people expect.'

Prayer idea: When others expect you to tease, ignore, be rude to someone or do things God wouldn't like, ask God to help you obey him rather them.

Turn back to God

Jeff looked serious. 'Hotshots, we didn't play well last match – let's work out why.'

'We're slow, not like we used to be,' commented Hong.
'We can't even throw straight – we're no good,' sighed Anna.

'Hold it, Hotshots!' Jeff put his hand up. 'We played badly and lost but we don't have to keep playing that way. The scores start from zero again next game, remember. We get a fresh start.'

John (often called John the Baptiser) told people they could have a fresh start too.

Read Luke 3:3-6

³ So John went along the Jordan Valley, telling the people, "Turn back to God and be baptised! Then your sins will be forgiven." ⁴ Isaiah the prophet wrote about John when he said,

"In the desert someone is shouting,
'Get the road ready for the Lord!
Make a straight path for him.
⁵ Fill up every valley
and level every mountain and hill.
Straighten the crooked paths
and smooth out the rough roads.
⁶ Then everyone will see the saving power of God.'"

Turn back to God (continued...)

People came to John to be baptised saying 'Sorry God for turning away from you.' They were sorry for everything they'd done wrong. Jesus was baptised yet he didn't need to say sorry. He'd never ever turned away from God.

Read Luke 3:21-22

²¹ While everyone else was being baptised, Jesus himself was baptised. Then as he prayed, the sky opened up, ²² and the Holy Spirit came down upon him in the form of a dove. A voice from heaven said, "You are my own dear Son, and I am pleased with you."

Prayer: *God, I'm sorry I turn away from you sometimes. Thank you for welcoming me again when I turn back. Help me to try to always please you.*

Think about the birth of Jesus

How long since you were born? ☐ years

How long since your mum was born? ☐ years

And your dad? ☐ years

How long is it since Jesus was born? Do you know what year it is now? Then you know approximately how long it is since Jesus was born. (It's not exact but it's close enough.)

☐☐☐☐ Write the year in the box. Now copy it on the Christmas gift tag on the next page.

7 It all begins with Jesus

Read Luke 2:1-7

[1] About that time Emperor Augustus gave orders for the names of all the people to be listed in record books. [2] These first records were made when Quirinius was governor of Syria.

[3] Everyone had to go to their own home town to be listed. [4] So Joseph had to leave Nazareth in Galilee and go to Bethlehem in Judea. Long ago Bethlehem had been King David's home town, and Joseph went there because he was from David's family.

[5] Mary was engaged to Joseph and travelled with him to Bethlehem. She was soon going to have a baby, [6] and while they were there, [7] she gave birth to her firstborn son. She dressed him in baby clothes and laid him on a bed of hay, because there was no room for them in the inn.

Write on this tag what year it is now (from the previous page).

So now we know that Jesus was born about ☐☐☐☐ years ago.

Our calendar starts from the time Jesus was born in Bethlehem. Jesus is that important!

Prayer: God, I wish I could see Jesus – it's hard to believe without seeing. Help me to know you are real.

Unbelievable things happen!

When he was little someone at school upset Sam. 'You'll never be a basketball player. You can't even bounce a ball.' Sam told his dad, who replied, 'I'm sure you could play if you want to.'

Sam trained hard and became one of the Hotshot's really good players. 'I'm glad I believed the right person,' he said.

What's the most unbelievable thing you've heard?

_____

Some shepherds were told one night about 2000 years ago that Jesus the Saviour had been born nearby. Do you think they believed that? ☐ Yes ☐ No

Read Luke 2:8-14

8 That night in the fields near Bethlehem some shepherds were guarding their sheep. 9 All at once an angel came down to them from the Lord, and the brightness of the Lord's glory flashed around them. The shepherds were frightened. 10 But the angel said, "Don't be afraid! I have good news for you, which will make everyone happy. 11 This very day in King David's home town a Saviour was born for you. He is Christ the Lord. 12 You will know who he is, because you will find him dressed in baby clothes and lying on a bed of hay."

13 Suddenly many other angels came down from heaven and joined in praising God. They said:

14 "Praise God in heaven!
Peace on earth to everyone who pleases God."

Pick two words that tell how the shepherds felt.

☐ excited   ☐ bored

☐ unbelieving   ☐ happy

☐ scared   ☐ worried

Would you have believed the angel about the baby's bed?

_____

What a place for God's Son!

Prayer: *Jesus, you are so great! Why did you choose to come to earth as a baby?*

'Going to church' in Bible times

When Jesus was a kid each town and village had a synagogue or meeting place. There was always something happening. Nearly every day the boys went to school at the synagogue to learn to read, write and recite God's law. Their teacher was called a 'rabbi'. Once a week, on the Sabbath (Saturday), people went to the synagogue to hear God's word, to sing and worship.

Everyone matters to God

'Hotshots, you're a great team!' Jeff told them as everyone began giving high fives, 'but there's one thing we need to watch out for. Some kids in this town think they're not important – a bit like those shepherds – but they are.'

'People looked down on shepherds in Jesus' time, because they were rough and poor and smelled of sheep. But guess who God told first about his Son?'

Read Luke 2:15-20

¹⁵ After the angels had left and gone back to heaven, the shepherds said to each other, "Let's go to Bethlehem and see what the Lord has told us about." ¹⁶ They hurried off and found Mary and Joseph, and they saw the baby lying on a bed of hay.

¹⁷ When the shepherds saw Jesus, they told his parents what the angel had said about him. ¹⁸ Everyone listened and was surprised. ¹⁹ But Mary kept thinking about all this and wondering what it meant.

²⁰ As the shepherds returned to their sheep, they were praising God and saying wonderful things about him. Everything they had seen and heard was just as the angel had said.

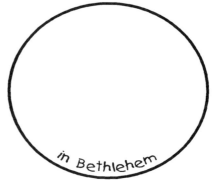

in Bethlehem

What did the shepherds see there?

Draw it in the frame.

Prayer: God, everyone matters to you. Thank you. Help me to show love to someone who feels left out or unimportant.

God keeps his promises

God promised long ago to send someone to save his people but nobody knew when. Simeon was certain it would be before he died because God's Spirit had told him. One day Simeon saw a baby and just knew it was the promised one.

Read Luke 2:25-33

25 At this time a man named Simeon was living in Jerusalem. Simeon was a good man. He loved God and was waiting for God to save the people of Israel. God's Spirit came to him 26 and told him that he wouldn't die until he had seen Christ the Lord.

27 When Mary and Joseph brought Jesus to the temple to do what the Law of Moses says should be done for a new baby, the Spirit told Simeon to go into the temple. 28 Simeon took the baby Jesus in his arms and praised God,

29 "Lord, I am your servant, and now I can die in peace, because you have kept your promise to me. 30 With my own eyes I have seen what you have done to save your people, 31 and foreign nations will also see this." ...

33 Jesus' parents were surprised at what Simeon had said.

Some old people know God very well and seem to shine with God's love. They listen to God and he tells them things. Simeon was like this. Unjumble these words that describe him?

doog

veldo Gdo

istleedn ot Gdo's Siirpt

dpeiasr Gdo

Prayer: Lord, we know that Jesus is the one who saves, but lots of people don't. Please help us to share the good news about him with others.

Some love Jesus, some don't

'Will the Hotshots ever be in the national league?' asked Anna.

'I'd love to be a professional!' exclaimed Dan.

'I'd rather be a teacher,' answered Anna, 'but I don't really know.'

Jeff was listening, 'You're all great kids. God has important work for each of you to do, now and when you are older.'

'What will it be?' asked Chris.

'Only God knows that, but you can start praying about it. Let's pray about it now.'

'God, most of the Hotshots don't know what they want to do later. Help them pick the better choices so that they can do good things for you. Thanks. Amen.'

Read Luke 2:36-38

³⁶ The prophet Anna was also there in the temple. She was the daughter of Phanuel from the tribe of Asher, and she was very old. In her youth she had been married for seven years, but her husband died. ³⁷ And now she was 84 years old. Night and day she served God in the temple by praying and often going without eating. ³⁸ At that time Anna came in and praised God. She spoke about the child Jesus to everyone who hoped for Jerusalem to be set free.

Simeon knew that Jesus would cause a sensation when he grew up – some would love him and others would want nothing to do with him.

Who else in the temple told people about Jesus? Clue: A member of the Hotshots has the same name.

She was an old lady who seemed to know God really well.

Prayer: *Turn Jeff's prayer into your prayer.*

God has a plan

The Hotshots were gloomy after playing the Slammers who beat them easily.

'It was terrible!' moaned Sam. 'They guessed exactly what would happen next. We didn't.'

'You're right,' Jeff agreed. 'The Slammers work hard at a game plan – they practise exactly what to do when each person gets the ball.'

'God has a plan too, but not about winning basketball. God always knew he would have to send Jesus to rescue people. In the Old Testament, God gave his people many clues about Jesus – Micah the prophet said where Jesus would be born 700 years before it happened!'

Write the name of the town in the boxes.

Now read Matthew 2:1-5

¹ When Jesus was born in the village of Bethlehem in Judea, Herod was king. During this time some wise men from the east came to Jerusalem ² and said, "Where is the child born to be king of the Jews? We saw his star in the east and have come to worship him."

³ When King Herod heard about this, he was worried, and so was everyone else in Jerusalem. ⁴ Herod brought together the chief priests and the teachers of the Law of Moses and asked them, "Where will the Messiah be born?"

⁵ They told him, "He will be born in Bethlehem, just as the prophet wrote."

Prayer: *God, it's hard to understand how you know about everything even before it happens, but I'm glad you do.*

13 You can't outsmart God

Read Matthew 2:7-12

⁷Herod secretly called in the wise men and asked them when they had first seen the star. ⁸He told them, "Go to Bethlehem and search carefully for the child. As soon as you find him, let me know. I want to go and worship him too."

⁹The wise men listened to what the king said and then left. And the star they had seen in the east went on ahead of them until it stopped over the place where the child was. ¹⁰They were thrilled and excited to see the star.

¹¹When the men went into the house and saw the child with Mary, his mother, they knelt down and worshipped him. They took out their gifts of gold, frankincense, and myrrh and gave them to him.

¹²Later they were warned in a dream not to return to Herod, and they went back home by another road.

Which picture looks like King Herod after he heard the news a new king was born. Circle it.

The king wanted to get rid of Jesus but didn't know where to look. He tried to trick the wise men into coming back and telling him where, but God was smarter than the king. What did God do? (Tick the right box.)

☐ killed the king
☐ warned the wise men not to return
☐ hid Jesus

'It's smart to be on God's side and to listen to his warnings.'

Prayer: *God, thank you that you're smarter than the bad guys. Help us to listen to your warnings – don't let us get caught up in bad things.*

Ships of the desert

Camels have been used on long journeys for thousands of years. Probably the wise men who came to worship Jesus did also.

Because camels carry people and cargo across the desert like ships across the sea, they are sometimes called 'ships of the desert'. Sometimes they make riders 'seasick' because of their rocking motion as they walk.

They have another use besides transport; they shed hair every spring which is woven into carpets and clothes.

Merchants have travelled along tracks in the desert for thousands of years. Their camels were piled high with goods for sale. Groups of people and animals crossed the desert together for protection from robbers and wild animals. These groups were called 'caravans'. Today, both cars and camels are used for transport in desert countries.

Camels
- Can walk in sand
- Travel slowly at 5 km/hour (3 miles/hour)
- Can change temperature of body when hot
- Can go a week without water
- Store fat in hump to use as food
- Can be stubborn, bad tempered and spit
- Can carry 250kg (550lb) of luggage.

4WD cars
- Tyres get bogged
- Travel fast – 100km/hr (62mph) or more
- Engines overheat in very hot weather
- Can be air conditioned
- Always need petrol, oil and water
- Don't spit or sit down when they please
- Can carry a lot of luggage
- Can carry 4 or 5 people

Which would you choose?

God keeps Jesus safe

Have you ever been in danger? What did you do? When the wise men tricked King Herod he tried even harder to get Jesus. Baby Jesus was in great danger!

Read Matthew 2:13-16

¹³ After the wise men had gone, an angel from the Lord appeared to Joseph in a dream and said, "Get up! Hurry and take the child and his mother to Egypt! Stay there until I tell you to return, because Herod is looking for the child and wants to kill him."

¹⁴ That night, Joseph got up and took his wife and the child to Egypt, ¹⁵ where they stayed until Herod died. So the Lord's promise came true, just as the prophet had said, "I called my son out of Egypt."

¹⁶ When Herod found out that the wise men from the east had tricked him, he was very angry. He gave orders for his men to kill all the boys who lived in or near Bethlehem and were two years old and younger. This was based on what he had learnt from the wise men.

What did the family do?

☐ bought a gun and got ready to fight

☐ ran away

'Sometimes it's best to escape trouble. God can help us escape. Other times it's best to stay and ask God for help and protection. Either way, God wants us to be safe and happy.'

Prayer: *God, thanks for being with me when there's danger. Show me how to keep safe.*

God does everything

"Good news! That huge centre in the Slammers team broke his arm. He's off for the rest of the season."

They knew it was unkind to be pleased but they couldn't help smiling, all except Chris. 'I hate to spoil things,' he said 'but his replacement is almost as big!' Everyone groaned.

'Don't panic, Hotshots,' said Jeff. 'Something like that happened to Jesus' family. The new King was nearly as bad as the old.'

Read Matthew 2:19-23

[19] After King Herod died, an angel from the Lord appeared in a dream to Joseph while he was still in Egypt. [20] The angel said, "Get up and take the child and his mother back to Israel. The people who wanted to kill him are now dead."

[21] Joseph got up and left with them for Israel. [22] But when he heard that Herod's son Archelaus was now ruler of Judea, he was afraid to go there. Then in a dream he was told to go to Galilee, [23] and they went to live there in the town of Nazareth.

Joseph was afraid but long ago God planned a spot where Jesus could grow up in safety.

Write down the first letter of each picture on the signpost and you'll see the name of the town.

Prayer: *Please God, whenever I'm scared, help me to remember that I'm never out of your sight.*

Growing like Jesus

'You've all grown since the start of the season,' said Jeff to the Hotshots.

'I wish you were right,' said Emily, 'but I'm still as short as when we started.'

'Not all of you have grown taller, but you have grown in other important ways.'

'Like what?'

'You're now a better team and what you know about the Bible has grown too.'

Read Luke 2:39-40

³⁹ After Joseph and Mary had done everything that the Law of the Lord commands, they returned home to Nazareth in Galilee. ⁴⁰ The child Jesus grew. He became strong and wise, and God blessed him.

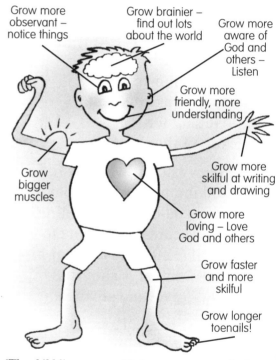

Jeff's sketch about different ways of growing

- Grow more observant – notice things
- Grow brainier – find out lots about the world
- Grow more aware of God and others – Listen
- Grow more friendly, more understanding
- Grow bigger muscles
- Grow more skilful at writing and drawing
- Grow more loving – Love God and others
- Grow faster and more skilful
- Grow longer toenails!

'The child Jesus grew. He became strong and wise, and God blessed him.'
Luke 2:40

Jeff sketched different ways of growing.

Tick the ways you would like to grow. Add some of your own.

- [ ] stronger
- [ ] friendlier
- [ ] prettier
- [ ] faster
- [ ] louder
- [ ] brainier
- [ ] braver
- [ ] _____
- [ ] kinder
- [ ] _____
- [ ] wiser
- [ ] _____

Prayer: God, you make everything grow. Please make me grow in ways that are good, just like Jesus.

Worshipping in the Temple

There were lots of synagogues in Palestine but only one Temple. Built in Jerusalem of white rock and decorated in gold, it was a huge, stunning building. The rabbis taught people that God lived there and called it 'the light of the earth'. Jews travelled hundreds of miles to worship God there, especially at festival time.

Its huge courtyard was open to everyone. There was a separate area just for Jews. When Jesus was older, he often talked there with the Jewish teachers. There was an inner area where only priests could serve (Zechariah led worship here – Luke 1:8). Furthest in was the tallest part of the Temple containing the Holy of Holies. The high priest was only allowed to go in there once a year to ask God to forgive him and all the people for anything they had done wrong.

Jesus goes on a holiday trip

Do you and your family enjoy special times at church like Carols by Candlelight, house parties, dawn services or anniversary dinners?

Jesus enjoyed special times too when he was growing up, like the Passover holiday. Jewish people celebrate this near the end of March. Jesus went to the temple in Jerusalem to celebrate Passover with his family and others from his village. Find out more about the temple on the next page.

Read Luke 2:41-45

41 Every year Jesus' parents went to Jerusalem for Passover. 42 And when Jesus was 12 years old, they all went there as usual for the celebration. 43 After Passover his parents left, but they didn't know that Jesus had stayed on in the city. 44 They thought he was travelling with some other people, and they went a whole day before they started looking for him. 45 When they couldn't find him with their relatives and friends, they went back to Jerusalem and started looking for him there.

When you are having a good time you don't realise what others are doing? That's what happened to Jesus. Guess what he was doing?

Prayer: Thank you for everyone who belongs to you. Thank you for the fun we have with our church family.

No jeans or burgers in Bible times

In Bible times, people wore the same clothes every day and almost never washed them. No one wore jeans or shorts. You wore a plain tunic unless you were very rich and put a cloak on top when it was cold. Clothes were home made by hand. This took a long time, so clothes were valuable.

Bread was the main food. Families also ate fruit and vegetables, fish, cheese, raisins and almonds. A special meal was roast lamb.

Only boys went to school. They learned their jobs from their fathers. Mothers taught girls how to care for the household and all about preparing food. One main job was bread making.

Houses were simple, made of stone or mud bricks. There was no glass in the windows, a dirt floor only – no carpet and little furniture. Windows were few, with no electric lights.

18 Jesus understands

Read Luke 2:46-50

⁴⁶ Three days later they found Jesus sitting in the temple, listening to the teachers and asking them questions. ⁴⁷ Everyone who heard him was surprised at how much he knew and at the answers he gave.

⁴⁸ When his parents found him, they were amazed. His mother said, "Son, why have you done this to us? Your father and I have been very worried, and we've been searching for you! ⁴⁹ Jesus answered, "Why did you have to look for me? Didn't you know that I would be in my Father's house?" ⁵⁰ But they did not understand what he meant.

Prayer: I'm glad you were once a child, so understand what it's like for me. Thanks Jesus.

'Cheer up Dan!'

'I can't!' complained Dan. 'I'm in trouble with Mum and Dad. I wasn't really bad. They just don't understand.'

'You and Jesus both,' said Jeff softly.

'Jesus? He never got into trouble!'

'Actually he did get into trouble with his parents when he was on holidays in Jerusalem.'

Jesus was told off for getting lost and making his parents worried. Jesus didn't think he was lost. What did he say? Draw a coloured line under the answer Jesus gave to his parents.

Who was his father? (You need two answers)

_____ and _____ .

19 Jesus and his parents

We know little about Jesus when he was growing up. Luke 2:51-52 gives us a clue about what he was like.

Luke 2:51-52

⁵¹ Jesus went back to Nazareth with his parents and obeyed them. His mother kept on thinking about all that had happened.

⁵² Jesus became wise, and he grew strong. God was pleased with him and so were the people.

Draw a circle around a word that shows Jesus' attitude to his parents.

Joseph was a carpenter. He probably made furniture, doors and yokes. A yoke is carved from wood and worn like a collar by two oxen or bullocks. It helps them pull heavy loads together. Jesus learned carpentry from his father, Joseph.

Colour in the yoke on these animals. Put a heavy wooden object that Jesus made in the back of the cart.

What job would you like to do when you grow up?
Unjumble these words for some jobs people do.

eaBkr ....
eeTarch ....
merblPu ....
denGarer ....
urerFm ....
Aasnttrou ....

Prayer: Please God, I want to live so that you and others are pleased with me. Help me to grow wise and strong like Jesus.

Jesus starts his special work

'When Jesus was growing up no one thought he was special. When they started to notice him he was about 30, quite old.'

What changed their mind?

Read Matthew 13:53-58

⁵³ When Jesus had finished telling these stories, he left ⁵⁴ and went to his home town. He taught in their meeting place, and the people were so amazed that they asked, "Where does he get all this wisdom and the power to work these miracles? ⁵⁵ Isn't he the son of the carpenter? Isn't Mary his mother, and aren't James, Joseph, Simon, and Judas his brothers? ⁵⁶ Don't his sisters still live here in our town? How can he do all this?" ⁵⁷ So the people were very unhappy because of what he was doing.

But Jesus said, "Prophets are honoured by everyone, except the people of their home town and their own family." ⁵⁸ And because the people didn't have any faith, Jesus didn't work many miracles there.

'So they thought Jesus was just like them and didn't believe he was God's Son.' said Dan. 'How stupid!'

'They missed out – if they'd believed, he would have done more for them, wouldn't he?' asked Sam.

Jeff was pleased the Hotshots were thinking hard, and smiled when Anna said, 'It's like that now – those who don't believe in Jesus miss out and never know what Jesus can do for them.'

'That's the way, team! You're growing in understanding – I'm proud of you.'

21 Jesus has a huge family

How many people are in your family? Write the numbers in the boxes and add them up. Ask Mum or Dad to help you.

- [ ] Parents
- [ ] Brothers
- [ ] Sisters
- [ ] Aunts & uncles
- [ ] Cousins
- [ ] Grandparents
- [ ] **Total**

But there's a much bigger family than Dan's!

Read Luke 8:19-21

[19] Jesus' mother and brothers went to see him, but because of the crowd they couldn't get near him. [20] Someone told Jesus, "Your mother and brothers are standing outside and want to see you."

[21] Jesus answered, "My mother and my brothers are those people who hear and obey God's message."

Anyone can join Jesus' family. What is the same about everyone in Jesus' family?

I've got the biggest family... Ten uncles and aunties and 36 cousins!

Follow the words on the circle over page to find out how to be one of Jesus' family.

Prayer: *Thank you God for the millions of people in your family. I'm glad it includes all sorts of people. It's good we don't have to talk the same language or look the same, but just need to obey God.*

Continued overpage

The buzz at the basketball

Start here → OBEYGOD'SMESSAGETHEYALLHEARAND

When the Hotshots turned up for practice, the senior team was on the court. 'Sorry I couldn't let you know earlier but we can't train here because the Bullets have changed practice times,' said Jeff, breaking the bad news.

'That's not fair! What about us?'
'I'm afraid it's a club rule. Senior teams get preference.'
'Hotshots will fall apart if we can't find another court!'
'It has to be here or I can't get to practice.'
'We'll never see each other again…'
'It'll be boring without Hotshots!'
'Hold it team!' Jeff broke in.

Psa

Philippians

Ma

I Timothy 2:8

I Thessalonians 5:17

Psalm 5:1

Psalm 28:6

v 7:7

'Are we going to moan and complain or can we *do* something?'
'What *can* we do? The Bullets are on our court!'
'I'll give you some clues. Look at these slips of paper that I prepared for our Bible time,' grinned Jeff as he gave them out.

They looked puzzled. When they realised they were Bible verses they went and looked them up in the club's Bibles. (Read them too if you have time, ticking each verse when you finish.)

After they finished reading, Jeff said, 'OK team, What are we going to do?'

'**Pray!**' they said together.
'Then let's do it now!'

'God, you know we need a practice court. Help us get one.'
'Sorry for complaining God…'
'Thanks for telling us to pray and thanks for hearing us.'
'Please help us to keep Hotshots going.'
'Thanks, Heavenly Father that we're your team and you know all about this.'

When they finished, Jeff announced, 'OK team. It's warm up time! We can do lots, even without a court.'

They jogged after Jeff – they couldn't think of a good reason not to warm up.

In the middle of stretches, the Bullets coach came over to talk to Jeff.

'This isn't going to work, Jeff. We need to go back to our old practice time. Looks like you get the court back.'

The Hotshots jumped up and cheered loudly.

'Wow!' said Hong under his breath.

'Thanks,' said Jeff to the coach. He looked up and grinned. So did everyone.

22 Keep praying

'From now on, I'm always going to pray!'

'Good plan. Now Isaac took 20 years to ask God for what he wanted! Let's read about it, and find out about God's double answer!'

Read Genesis 25:19-21, 24-26

[19] Isaac was the son of Abraham, [20] and he was 40 years old when he married Rebekah, the daughter of Bethuel. She was also the sister of Laban, the Aramean from northern Syria.

Almost 20 years later, [21] Rebekah still had no children. So Isaac asked the LORD to let her have a child, and the LORD answered his prayer...

[24] When Rebekah gave birth, [25] the first baby was covered with red hair, so he was named Esau. [26] The second baby grabbed on to his brother's heel, so they named him Jacob. Isaac was 60 years old when they were born.

What did Isaac ask for?
- [ ] money
- [ ] a house
- [ ] a baby

If you are worrying or complaining about something, it is **always** better to pray. Talk to God about it now.

Prayer: Lord, thank you that you always hear my prayers. Help me to trust that you know best.

Everyone is different

Jeff asked for ideas for a special Hotshots day during the school holidays. There were lots of suggestions – pizza and videos, hot dogs and outdoor games, tabloid sports and party food.

The Hotshots like different things. So do people in the Bible.

Read Genesis 25:27-28

27 As Jacob and Esau grew older, Esau liked the outdoors and became a good hunter, while Jacob settled down and became a shepherd. 28 Esau would take the meat of wild animals to his father Isaac, and so Isaac loved him more, but Jacob was his mother's favourite son.

Who understands you best?
Who do you disagree with?
How can you make family life happier?

Write their names under the pictures.

Prayer:
Loving God,
when I find it hard to get along happily with people, help me to understand others and try to please them, not just myself. Help them to think of others too.

24 Families are important

In many countries the oldest child gets special rights just because they are the oldest – like Esau, who was the oldest twin. He'd be the head of the family when his father died. Did he take that seriously?

Do the older kids at your place have extra rights too?

Read Genesis 25:29-34

²⁹ One day, Jacob was cooking some stew, when Esau came home hungry ³⁰ and said, "I'm starving to death! Give me some of that red stew right now!" That's how Esau got the name "Edom."

³¹ Jacob replied, "Sell me your rights as the firstborn son."

³² "I'm about to die," Esau answered. "What good will those rights do me?"

³³ But Jacob said, "Promise me your birthrights, here and now!" And that's what Esau did. ³⁴ Jacob then gave Esau some bread and some of the bean stew, and when Esau had finished eating and drinking, he just got up and left, showing how little he thought of his rights as the firstborn.

Esau didn't care about his family; he cared only about himself.

In the fish, write a word that describes a person who cares very little about others.

Prayer: *Heavenly Father, thank you for my family. Please help me to be unselfish. Help my family to be unselfish too. What can I do to make my family the way you would like it to be?*

Act the truth

There was a mix up in the scores. Some of Sam's goals were recorded against Dan.

'We need to put the mistake right,' said Jeff.

'Are you sure we can?' asked Dan hopefully. 'It's already in the book.'

'Mistakes can be corrected,' said Jeff firmly. 'You'll be acting like Jacob if you keep Sam's points – that caused all sorts of trouble.'

Read Genesis 27:1-10

¹After Isaac had become old and almost blind, he called in his firstborn son Esau, who asked him, "Father, what can I do for you?"

² Isaac replied, "I am old and might die at any time. ³ So take your bow and arrows, then go out in the fields, and kill a wild animal. ⁴ Cook some of that tasty food that I love so much and bring it to me. I want to eat it once more and give you my blessing before I die."

⁵ Rebekah had been listening, and as soon as Esau left to go hunting, ⁶ she said to Jacob, ... "⁸ Now, my son, listen carefully to what I want you to do. ⁹ Go and kill two of your best young goats and bring them to me. I'll cook the tasty food that your father loves so much. ¹⁰ Then you can take it to him, so he can eat it and give you his blessing before he dies."

Jacob and his mum plotted to act a lie.

Put the words in the right order to find the mystery message:

'a lie/Acting/bad/telling/is as/as/one'

_____

Prayer: God, please help me to live the truth by what I say and do.

Cheating causes trouble

Read Genesis 27:15-20

15 [Rebekah] took Esau's best clothes and put them on Jacob. 16 She covered the smooth part of his hands and neck with goatskins 17 and gave him some bread and the tasty food she had cooked.

18 Jacob went to his father and said, "Father, here I am."

"Which one of my sons are you?" his father asked.

19 Jacob replied, "I am Esau, your firstborn, and I have done what you told me. Please sit up and eat the meat I have brought. Then you can give me your blessing."

20 Isaac asked, "My son, how did you find an animal so quickly?"

"The LORD your God was kind to me," Jacob answered.

Jacob cheated his dad by pretending he was Esau. Rebekah cheated Jacob by pretending to him it was OK to act out a lie.

Prayer: Dear God, it's horrible to hear that people hurt their family or friends. Help me to be honest with everyone I know and never deceive anyone.

27 Dirty tricks

Poor old Isaac couldn't see. Nor could he see the dirty tricks being played by his wife and son.

Read Genesis 27:21-26,28

21 "My son," Isaac said, "come closer, where I can touch you and find out if you really are Esau." 22 Jacob went closer. His father touched him and said, "You sound like Jacob, but your hands feel hairy like Esau's." 23 And so Isaac blessed Jacob, thinking he was Esau.

24 Isaac asked, "Are you really my son Esau?"

"Yes, I am," Jacob answered.

25 So Isaac told him, "Serve me the wild meat, and I can give you my blessing."

Jacob gave him some meat, and he ate it. He also gave him some wine, and he drank it. 26 Then Isaac said... 28 "God will bless you, my son, with dew from heaven and with fertile fields, rich with grain and grapes."

When Isaac used these words to bless Jacob he hoped God would make them true for him. What words could you say to bring blessing to people?

You could make a blessing card such as 'Get well soon' or 'Have a great day'. While making it, pray for the person who will receive it.

Prayer: Lord, thank you for blessing me and help me to be a blessing to others.

28 Guard your reputation

'We're playing the Busters next. It's no fun,' said Chris. 'They push and shove, pretend it's an accident and say mean things. It's time the Hotshots got rough too!'

'We don't want to be called cheats and shovers!' declared Sam.

'That's right Sam,' said Jeff. 'We have a good reputation for playing fair while having fun. Why trade the name Hotshots for Bad Sports?'

'Jacob' sounds like 'cheat' in the Hebrew language. Would you like a name like that?

Read Genesis 27:30-36

30 Right after Isaac had given Jacob his blessing and Jacob had gone, Esau came back from hunting. 31 He cooked the tasty food, brought it to his father, and said, "Father, please sit up and eat the meat I have brought you, so you can give me your blessing."

32 "Who are you?" Isaac asked.

"I am Esau, your first-born son."

33 Isaac started trembling and said, "Then who brought me some wild meat right before you came in? I ate it and gave him a blessing that cannot be taken back."

34 Esau cried loudly and begged, "Father, give me a blessing too!"

35 Isaac answered, "Your brother tricked me and stole your blessing."

36 Esau replied, "My brother deserves the name Jacob, because he has already cheated me twice. The first time he cheated me out of my rights as the first-born son, and now he has cheated me out of my blessing."

How would you like others to think of you?

☐ fair   ☐ funny

☐ mean   ☐ stuck up

☐ helpful ☐ lazy

Prayer: Please God, help me to guard my good name and to think before I act.

Telling tales

'Jeff, Anna just said that Hong thinks Chris isn't trying…'

'Stop right there!' said Jeff, calling the Hotshots together.

'Team! There's no room in this team for telling tales, even true ones. They cause trouble. You'll see what I mean when we read about Jacob's children.'

Read Genesis 37:1-4

¹ Jacob lived in the land of Canaan, where his father Isaac had lived, ² and this is the story of his family.

When Jacob's son Joseph was 17 old, he took care of the sheep with his brothers, the sons of Bilhah and Zilpah. But he was always telling his father all sorts of bad things about his brothers.

³ Jacob loved Joseph more than he did any of his other sons, because Joseph was born after Jacob was very old. Jacob had given Joseph a fancy coat ⁴ to show that he was his favourite son, and so Joseph's brothers hated him and would not be friendly to him.

Joseph's many stepbrothers were much older than him. Joseph kept telling tales on them probably because he felt left out. Find 3 sad things about this family in the stripes on Joseph's coat.

Prayer: Thank you that words can make people happy, not just sad and grumpy. Please help me to think before I speak and not say anything stupid, even if it's true.

30 Being a leader

Read Genesis 37:5-11

⁵ One day, Joseph told his brothers what he had dreamt and they hated him even more. ⁶ Joseph said, "Let me tell you about my dream. ⁷ We were out in the field, tying up bundles of wheat. Suddenly my bundle stood up, and your bundles gathered around and bowed down to it."

⁸ His brothers asked, "Do you really think you are going to be king and rule over us?" Now they hated Joseph more than ever because of what he had said about his dream.

⁹ Joseph later had another dream, and he told his brothers, "Listen to what else I dreamt. The sun, the moon, and eleven stars bowed down to me."

¹⁰ When he told his father about this dream, his father became angry and said, "What's that supposed to mean? Are your mother and I and your brothers all going to come and bow down in front of you?" ¹¹ Joseph's brothers were jealous of him, but his father kept wondering about the dream.

Joseph believed he would be a leader over his brothers and parents. Good leaders help everyone feel important but Joseph only wanted to tell everyone how much better he was than them.

Tick the right boxes.
Do you like telling others you are better than them?
☐ YES   ☐ NO
Do you like others hinting they are better than you?
☐ YES   ☐ NO
Decode the secret message from Philippians 2:3.

Prayer: *Please, help me to see myself as you see me – no better, no worse than them.*

Joseph did what his Dad asked

Read Genesis 37:12-14

¹² One day when Joseph's brothers had taken the sheep to a pasture near Shechem, ¹³ his father Jacob said to him, "I want you to go to your brothers. They are with the sheep near Shechem."

"Yes, sir," Joseph answered.

¹⁴ His father said, "Go and find out how your brothers and the sheep are doing. Then come back and let me know." So he sent him from Hebron Valley.

Perhaps Joseph tried to get out of it when his dad asked him to go and find his brothers.

Prayer: Lord God, please help me to obey my parents, even when it's a lot of effort and I don't want to.

Joseph left and found his brothers in Dothan.

Shechem was nearly 100km away. It would be a long walk – no cars or bikes then. And it would probably be boring when he got there. But Joseph obeyed his father. How long would it take for Joseph to get to Shechem if he walked 20km a day?

Draw or write about something your parents want you to do but you don't often do.

I mightn't be coming next week – I have to go out with the family but I don't want to go. I'm trying to talk Dad out of it.

32 It's not fair!

When you do the right thing you expect things to go well. But it doesn't always happen that way.

Joseph obeyed his father and went to find his brothers. Then things got worse.

Read Genesis 37:18-24

[18] But before he got there, they saw him coming and made plans to kill him. [19] They said to one another, "Look, here comes the hero of those dreams! [20] Let's kill him and throw him into a pit and say that some wild animal ate him. Then we'll see what happens to those dreams."
[21] Reuben heard this and tried to protect Joseph from them. "Let's not kill him," he said. [22] "Don't murder him or even harm him. Just throw him into a dry well out here in the desert." Reuben planned to rescue Joseph later and take him back to his father.
[23] When Joseph came to his brothers, they pulled off his fancy coat [24] and threw him into a dry well.

'Those brothers were horrible to Joseph. Why didn't God stop them?'

'You can't blame God. The brothers were bad. *They* did it.'

'Maybe God did stop them. They were going to kill Joseph, remember?'

Jeff smiled. 'God certainly knew what was happening. You'll enjoy the rest of the story.'

Prayer: *God, sometimes it's hard to understand why you let bad things happen. When others are mean to me, please help me to trust you.*

33 From bad to worse

"I'd like to get rid of my brother's old coat – I hate wearing it."

"I wish I could lose last year's bad school report."

"I wish next door's dog would get lost! It barks all night."

"I wish the rug I spilled cordial on could be thrown away. Mum can't get the stain out."

Don't you sometimes wish you could get rid of some things and never see them again?

Joseph annoyed his brothers so much they wanted to get rid of him. Even though this was wrong it didn't bother them.

Prayer: *God, some people do terrible things. Please keep me safe. Help me never to do things to hurt others.*

Read Genesis 37:25-28

25 As Joseph's brothers sat down to eat, they looked up and saw a group of Ishmaelites coming from Gilead. Their camels were loaded with all kinds of spices that they were taking to Egypt. 26 So Judah said, "What will we gain if we kill our brother and hide his body? 27 Let's sell him to the Ishmaelites and not harm him. After all, he is our brother." And the others agreed. 28 When the Midianite merchants came by, Joseph's brothers took him out of the well, and for 20 pieces of silver they sold him to the Ishmaelites who took him to Egypt.

Where's my mummy!

If you fly over Egypt you will see big cities with palm trees, sandy deserts and pyramids. These huge stone pyramids are so old. They were even there when Joseph was taken to Egypt long ago.

The river Nile is the longest river in the world. It flows for about 4600 km. For 6000 years it has watered crops in Egypt. Papyrus reeds, which are used to make paper, still grow along its banks. Crocodiles live amongst the reeds.

Egypt's kings were called 'Pharaohs'. They were very rich and powerful. When they died their bodies were preserved. These were called 'mummies' – nothing to do with families! First the insides of the dead body were taken out. Then the body was wrapped in strips of cloth soaked with special chemicals to preserve it. Scientists called archaeologists have found some of these mummies. They are thousands of years old, still in their original boxes. These were beautifully decorated with gold and jewels.

Egypt was once the greatest country in the world. It had great cities with palaces and luxury houses. Slaves did all the work for the Egyptians at home and much of the building and farming too. Slaves lived hard and miserable lives.

The 'cheating' web

Remember how Jacob deceived his old father? Check back on pages 39-42 if you've forgotten. Now, Jacob's *sons* deceived *him*!

Read Genesis 37:29-35

29 When Reuben returned to the well and didn't find Joseph there, he tore his clothes in sorrow. 30 Then he went back to his brothers and said, "The boy is gone! What am I going to do?"

31 Joseph's brothers killed a goat and dipped Joseph's fancy coat in its blood. 32 After this, they took the coat to their father and said, "We found this! Look at it carefully and see if it belongs to your son."

33 Jacob knew it was Joseph's coat and said, "It's my son's coat! Joseph has been torn to pieces and eaten by some wild animal."

34 Jacob mourned for Joseph a long time, and to show his sorrow he tore his clothes and wore sackcloth. 35 All of Jacob's children came to comfort him, but he refused to be comforted.

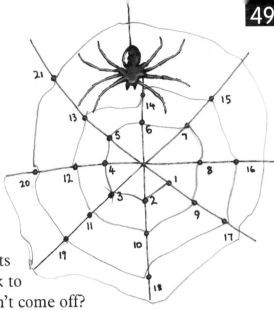

Have you ever walked into a spider's web? Did you find bits of the web stuck to you that wouldn't come off?

Cheating is like that. When you deceive others you have to tell lies. These keep getting bigger. The only way out is to own up then ask people to forgive you. You should then make sure you don't do it again.

Join the dots to make a cheating spider's web.

Prayer: *Thank you for honest people who speak and live the truth. Please help me to be like that too.*

A walking talking blessing

How would you like to be a slave like Joseph was? He couldn't change this so he tried to be the best slave he could. (Read more about slaves on page 51.)

We often find ourselves in bad situations but we can choose how we act.

Read Genesis 39:1-6

¹ The Ishmaelites took Joseph to Egypt and sold him to Potiphar, the king's official in charge of the palace guard. ²⁻³ So Joseph lived in the home of Potiphar, his Egyptian owner.

Soon Potiphar realized that the LORD was helping Joseph to be successful in whatever he did. ⁴ Potiphar liked Joseph and made him his personal assistant, putting him in charge of his house and all of his property. ⁵ Because of Joseph, the LORD began to bless Potiphar's family and fields. ⁶ Potiphar left everything up to Joseph, and with Joseph there, the only decision he had to make was what he wanted to eat.

☐ We can say 'It's not fair' and sulk or be angry. (This will make everyone miserable, including ourselves.) ... or...

☐ We can try to make the best of the situation.

Tick what Joseph did. Tick what God would want you to do next time things go wrong for you.

Prayer idea: *Think of a time when you could have acted like Joseph but didn't. You could say sorry to God and ask God to help you next time things go wrong.*

Slaves for sale

These days we find it hard to believe that human beings could be sold in a market. But that is what happened.

Thousands of years after Joseph lived, the apostle Paul told slaves how Jesus would want them to behave. Read **Colossians 3:22-23** to see what he said.

22 Slaves, you must always obey your earthly masters. Try to please them at all times, and not just when you think they are watching. Honour the Lord and serve your masters with your whole heart. 23 Do your work willingly, as though you were serving the Lord himself, and not just your earthly master.

You can volunteer to be a slave for a day! Think of some task that you can offer as a gift. Offer them to your parents, your grandparents, your friends, your neighbour or someone at your church. You could ask them to pay some money to a charity.

Here are some ideas.

Joseph could be trusted?

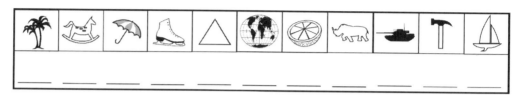

Read Genesis 39:6-12, 16-18

⁶ Joseph was well-built and handsome, ⁷ and Potiphar's wife soon noticed him. She asked him to make love to her, ⁸ but he refused and said, "My master isn't worried about anything in his house, because he has placed me in charge of everything he owns. ⁹ … I won't sin against God by doing such a terrible thing as this." ¹⁰ She kept begging Joseph day after day, but he refused to do what she wanted or even to go near her.

¹¹ One day, Joseph went to Potiphar's house to do his work, and none of the other servants were there. ¹² Potiphar's wife grabbed hold of his coat and said, "Make love to me!" Joseph ran out of the house, leaving her hanging onto his coat…

¹⁶ Potiphar's wife kept Joseph's coat until her husband came home. ¹⁷ Then she said, "That Hebrew slave of yours tried to rape me! ¹⁸ But when I screamed for help, he left his coat and ran out of the house."

Potiphar's wife was rich and powerful. If Joseph had done what she wanted she could have made life easy for Joseph. He said 'No' to her because it was wrong and because his master trusted him.

Write the first letter of each picture to make a long word. It means 'can be trusted'.

Can people trust you to do what is right and speak the truth? God can always be trusted. We can trust him to be with us and care for us and keep his promises.

Prayer: *Thanks God that you are 100 per cent trustworthy. Remind me to be trustworthy too whenever I think of lying or doing something wrong.*

37 Framed

Western movies sometimes say someone has been framed – that is, blamed for something he did not do. Joseph was framed!

Genesis 39: 19-23

19 Potiphar became very angry 20 and threw Joseph into the same prison where the king's prisoners were kept.

While Joseph was in prison, 21 the LORD helped him and was good to him. He even made the jailer like Joseph so much that 22 he put him in charge of the other prisoners and of everything that was done in the jail. 23 The jailer did not worry about anything, because the LORD was with Joseph and made him successful in all that he did.

'Life isn't always fair. Sometimes we have to put up with tough times and keep trusting God until things get better.'

Things kept going wrong for Joseph, even though he trusted God and was good. God has made us a promise for times like that. To discover it, read these words that are upside down.

"We know that God is always working for the good of everyone who loves him."
Romans 8:28

Prayer: Father God, thank you for being with me in the tough times. Never let me forget that you are with me. You know what's going on and that good things will come out of it.

Did Joseph stay in prison? Read on...

The king of Egypt was upset because he had a dream he didn't understand. He was told that Joseph could tell the future from dreams. So the king sent to the prison for him.

'I don't know what dreams mean,' said Joseph. 'Only God knows.'

When the king described his dream, God told Joseph what it meant. This is what Joseph told the king:

'After 7 years of large crops, there will be 7 years famine. You need to find someone to set up a program to save food in the 7 good years or people will starve.'

The king said to his officials, 'Joseph's the best man for that job!'

Joseph did a wonderful job. By the time the dry weather came, more than enough food was stored in Egypt. People from countries where there was no food travelled there to buy some.

ACROSS
1. His brothers were jealous
3. Isaac did this to Jacob (see page 41)
5. How many sons of Jacob?
6. The brother who said not to kill Joseph
8. The well was ___
9. 'Jacob' sounds like ___ (see page 42)

DOWN
2. Where Joseph looked for his brothers
3. Joseph had eleven ___
4. Joseph became a ___ to Potiphar
7. Joseph was taken to which country?
8. Joseph told his family about his ___
9. Jacob gave Joseph a fancy ___

*Among these were Joseph's brothers. Although they didn't recognise him, Joseph knew who they were. He teased them and gave them a hard time. Eventually he told them who he was and arranged for the whole family to live in Egypt to stop them from starving. (Read the full story in **Genesis 45:1-8**)*

The brothers felt bad about the way they had treated Joseph but he told them, 'You tried to harm me but God made it turn out for the best so that he could save all these people.'

Answers to puzzle on page 57.

38. Things change

Do you know an old person who loves God? Ask them what things God has done for them, but don't be surprised if they've forgotten most of them!

Read Exodus 1:1-10

1-5 When Jacob went to Egypt, his son Joseph was already there. So Jacob took his eleven other sons and their families. They were: Reuben, Simeon, Levi, Judah, Issachar, Zebulun, Benjamin, Dan, Naphtali, Gad, and Asher. Altogether, Jacob had 70 children, grandchildren, and great-grandchildren who went with him.

6 After Joseph, his brothers, and everyone else in that generation had died, **7** the people of Israel became so numerous that the whole region of Goshen was full of them.

8 Many years later a new king came to power. He didn't know what Joseph had done for Egypt, **9** and he told the Egyptians:

There are too many of those Israelites in our country, and they are becoming more powerful than we are. **10** If we don't outsmart them, their families will keep growing larger. And if our country goes to war, they could easily fight on the side of our enemies and escape from Egypt.

What good things has God done for you, your church or your family? Write a couple of them down. Dan keeps his list on his computer so he won't forget and Jeff's mum writes them in a special book.

Prayer: *Lord God, you have done so many good things for so many people. Thanks for your goodness to us all.*

Make your own spinx

In ancient Egypt they used to build sphinxes with an animal body and a human head. They reminded them of their famous kings.

Copy this picture to make your own sphinx. At the bottom of it, write what you want to remember. The Hotshots wrote different things on theirs:

Hong – 'God works things out for those who love him.'

Emily – 'Don't worry – God is here.'

Sam – 'God is with me in good times and bad times.'

Kim – 'Remember what God has done.'

Jeff – 'Don't forget to remember!'

Anna – 'Be trustworthy, God is.'

Dan – 'Smile. God is here.'

Answers to crossword on page 55: Across: 1. Joseph; 3. Blessed; 5. Twelve; 6. Reuben; 8. Dry; 9. Cheat
Down: 2. Shechem; 3. Brothers; 4. Slave; 7. Egypt; 8. Dreams; 9. Coat

39 Life can be tough

"Things are bad at home now, my mum's been in hospital and school's no fun any more. Everything's bad."

"Things change. We all have tough times and good times. I know 3 things that can help."

1. Lookforwardtothingsgettingbetter
2. Rememberthegoodtimesinthepastandsmile!
3. AskGodtohelpyouliveforhiminthehardtimes

Find the 3 things Jeff told Hong.
Draw lines to separate the words.

Read Exodus 1:11-14

¹¹ The Egyptians put slave bosses in charge of the people of Israel and tried to wear them down with hard work. Those bosses forced them to build the cities of Pithom and Rameses, where the king could store his supplies. ¹² But even though the Israelites were mistreated, their families grew larger, and they took over more land. Because of this, the Egyptians hated them more than before ¹³ and made them work so hard ¹⁴ that their lives were miserable. The Egyptians were cruel to the people of Israel and forced them to make bricks and to mix mortar and to work in the fields.

The Egyptians forgot about Joseph. They forgot how he saved their country. The Hebrew people didn't forget – they made sure they told their children and grandchildren so it would never be forgotten.

Why did the Hebrew people feel miserable?
_____

Why were the Egyptians worried?
_____

Prayer: Thank you God for being with us in good times and bad times.

40 They respected God

Read Exodus 1:15-22

15 Finally, the king called in Shiphrah and Puah, the two women who helped the Hebrew mothers when they gave birth. 16 He told them, "If a Hebrew woman gives birth to a girl, let the child live. If the baby is a boy, kill him!"

17 But the two women were faithful to God and did not kill the boys, even though the king had told them to. 18 The king called them in again and asked, "Why are you letting those baby boys live?"

19 They answered, "Hebrew women have their babies much quicker than Egyptian women. By the time we arrive, their babies are already born." 20–21 God was good to the two women because they truly respected him, and he blessed them with children of their own.

'I hope no powerful person ever tells me to do the wrong thing.'

'They probably will,' Jeff continued.

'Like when Ben's brother wanted me to nick something at the markets,' said Sam.

Jeff looked serious. 'When something like that happens to me, I try to imagine that Jesus is standing beside me. Then it's easier to do what Jesus wants because he's right there.'

What wrong things might someone expect you to do? How can you make sure you won't give in to them?

Prayer: Lord, please help me to respect you. Let me try to please you more than anyone else.

A family working together

Read Exodus 2:1–4

[1] A man from the Levi tribe married a woman from the same tribe, [2] and she later had a baby boy. He was a beautiful child, and she kept him inside for three months. [3] But when she could no longer keep him hidden, she made a basket out of reeds and covered it with tar. She put him in the basket and placed it in the tall grass along the edge of the Nile River. [4] The baby's older sister stood off at a distance to see what would happen to him.

This family loved their precious baby boy. They didn't want to throw him into the Nile. What could they do?

God gave them an idea – get one of the Egyptian princesses to adopt their baby. Then he would be safe. If only she could see him, surely she'd want him then. So they planned this to happen.

What did the mother make? Draw it floating on the river and draw Miriam hiding.

Prayer: It's great God, that kids can be part of your plan. Show me what you want me to do. Make me brave enough to do it.

Partners!

Read Exodus 2:5-10

⁵ About that time one of the king's daughters came down to take a bath in the river, while her servant women walked along the river bank. She saw the basket in the tall grass and sent one of the young women to pull it out of the water. ⁶ When the king's daughter opened the basket, she saw the baby and felt sorry for him because he was crying.
She said, "This must be one of the Hebrew babies."

⁷ At once the baby's older sister came up and asked, "Do you want me to get a Hebrew woman to take care of the baby for you?"

⁸ "Yes," the king's daughter answered.

So the girl brought the baby's mother, ⁹ and the king's daughter told her, "Take care of this child, and I will pay you."

The baby's mother carried him home and took care of him. ¹⁰ And when he was old enough, she took him to the king's daughter, who adopted him. She named him Moses because she said, "I pulled him out of the water."

What an amazing solution to a huge problem!

'God works things out and sometimes does a miracle to change things. But at other times he works through ordinary people who pray, plan and do what they think is best.'

Jeff talked with the Hotshots about problems and how God uses kids just like them to make a difference.

Continued overpage

Partners! (continued...)

Hong prayed for his mum who was often tired and looked sad. He started to notice things to do that could help her or make her feel brighter. He's hoping his brother will help too.

Emily prayed for a new girl at school who had no friends. Now they are both friends and Emily hopes she'll join Hotshots soon.

Chris was worried about pollution. He talked to a teacher and now they've started a 'Care for the Earth' group at school.

Prayer: *Thank you God that we can be partners with you, working out your plans. Please help me not to give up when things seem too hard. Make me keen to work with you.*

43 Who do you think you are?

The Hotshots were practising passing shots. They were not doing well.

'Hold it Hotshots!' Jeff's voice was loud and firm. 'We're here to have fun and it doesn't look like we're having much! Stop now and read the next part of the Moses story. Dan and Anna will be very interested,' he grinned.

Read Exodus 2:11-15

¹¹ After Moses had grown up, he went out to where his own people were hard at work, and he saw an Egyptian beating one of them. ¹² Moses looked around to see if anyone was watching, then he killed the Egyptian and hid his body in the sand.

¹³ When Moses went out the next day, he saw two Hebrews fighting. So he went to the man who had started the fight and asked, "Why are you beating up one of your own people?"

¹⁴ The man answered, "Who put you in charge of us and made you our judge? Are you planning to kill me, just as you killed that Egyptian?"

This frightened Moses because he was sure that people must have found out what had happened. ¹⁵ When the king heard what Moses had done, the king wanted to kill him. But Moses escaped and went to the land of Midian.

Although Moses was adopted into an Egyptian family he knew he was a Hebrew. So why wouldn't the two

Continued overpage

Who do you think you are? (Continued)

Hebrew slaves listen to Moses? Did he think he was better than them? Were they jealous of his easy life? They didn't keep Moses' secret so he had to run for his life.

What other Hebrew escaped from a king who wanted to kill him? CLUE: See page 24.

_____

_____

Prayer idea:
Are there people who won't listen to you? Can you work out why? Do you act as if you are better than them? Are they jealous of you? Can you do anything to make friends?

If you are growing too old for Hotshots ...

... try *Snapshots!*

There's a Bible section for every day.
There are puzzles and activities.
You can subscribe to receive Snapshots every quarter.

Being helpful

Moses ran away to another country called Midian to escape arrest. He had no friends or family nearby so it was probably hard for him. Moses had problems but could still be helpful to others!

Read Exodus 2:15-19

15 But Moses escaped and went to the land of Midian.

One day, Moses was sitting there by a well, 16 when the seven daughters of Jethro, the priest of Midian, came up to water their father's sheep and goats. 17 Some shepherds tried to chase them away, but Moses came to their rescue and watered their animals. 18 When Jethro's daughters returned home, their father asked, "Why have you come back so early today?"

19 They answered, "An Egyptian rescued us from the shepherds, and he even watered our sheep and goats."

Prayer:
Lord God, when things are going wrong for me I often feel tired and upset and only think about myself. Please help me to think of others and be helpful even when I don't feel like it.

"I'm so proud of you Emily. Even though you're disappointed you didn't get chosen for the school team you're still kind and thoughtful to others. Some children are awful to others when they are unhappy."

How did Moses help the seven women?

EH DETCETORP MEHT

EH DERETAW RIEHT SLAMINA

45 Deep down inside

Read Exodus 3:1-5

¹ One day, Moses was taking care of the sheep and goats of his father-in-law Jethro, the priest of Midian, and Moses decided to lead them across the desert to Sinai, the holy mountain. ² There an angel of the LORD appeared to him from a burning bush. Moses saw that the bush was on fire, but it wasn't burning up. ³ "This is strange!" he said to himself. "I'll go over and see why the bush isn't burning up."

⁴ When the LORD saw Moses coming near the bush, he called him by name, and Moses answered, "Here I am."

⁵ God replied, "Don't come any closer. Take off your sandals—the ground where you are standing is holy."

'Has God ever spoken to you, Jeff?' Dan asked, but everyone wanted to know.

Jeff nodded.

'What was it like? Thunder?'

'It's hard to explain,' said Jeff thoughtfully. 'God has spoken to me quite a few times but not really in a voice you could hear.'

'Huh? What is it like then?'

'Well, last week I was annoyed at my friend. I was really angry. I picked up the phone to say something nasty but in my mind I could hear God telling me to watch the words I used or I'd make things worse.'

Deep down inside (continued ...)

'God told me to start up Hotshots. I had no idea if anyone would join, but God let me know that he'd send along enough kids for a team.'

'He did? How did you know?'

'Deep down inside I just knew that it was God.

Has God ever talked to you? Do you listen for him?

Prayer: Thank you for listening when I pray to you. I'd really like you to speak to me. Please help me to listen so that when you have something to say to me I don't miss it.

What God said to Moses

Read Exodus 3:6-8a

⁶ I am the God who was worshipped by your ancestors Abraham, Isaac, and Jacob."

Moses was afraid to look at God, and so he hid his face.

⁷ The Lord said:

"I have seen how my people are suffering as slaves in Egypt, and I have heard them beg for my help because of the way they are being mistreated. I feel sorry for them, ⁸ and I have come down to rescue them from the Egyptians."

46. God speaks to Moses

Read Exodus 3:8-10

"I will bring my people out of Egypt into a country where there is good land, rich with milk and honey. I will give them the land where the Canaanites, Hittites, Amorites, Perizzites, Hivites, and Jebusites now live. ⁹ My people have begged for my help, and I have seen how cruel the Egyptians are to them. ¹⁰ Now go to the king! I am sending you to lead my people out of his country."

I still don't understand how God can talk to people

You have to listen, but not with your ears. Sounds weird doesn't it, but it's not. Inside all of us there is a quiet spot—our spirit. God speaks to our spirit.

Prayer:
Thank you that you hear me when I pray. Please help me to be patient when you don't seem to answer. Help me to trust you anyway.

Put the right words in the spaces.

The _____ were cruel to the Hebrew _____. The slaves _____ for help. Nothing seemed to happen but God had _____. He sent _____ to _____ them.

rescue   slaves   prayed   Moses   heard   Egyptians

Moses was probably now about 80 years old! Ancient! Hardly a Mini-star any more! Let's leave him now and move on to a much younger person.

47 Stop feeling sad

'Hey team!' Jeff smiled, pulling out a board with writing on it. 'There's some things you need to know before we start reading about this new Mini-star.' Can you help the Hotshots fill in the gaps?

Read 1 Samuel 16:1-5

¹ One day he said, "Samuel, I've rejected Saul, and I refuse to let him be king any longer. Stop feeling sad about him. Put some olive oil in a small container and go and visit a man named Jesse, who lives in Bethlehem. I've chosen one of his sons to be my king."

² Samuel answered, "If I do that, Saul will find out and have me killed."

"Take a calf with you," the LORD replied. "Tell everyone that you've come to offer it as a sacrifice to me, ³ then invite Jesse to the sacrifice. When I show you which one of his sons I have chosen, pour the olive oil on his head."

⁴ Samuel did what the LORD told him and went to Bethlehem. The town leaders went to meet him, but they were terribly afraid and asked, "Is this a friendly visit?"

⁵ "Yes, it is!" Samuel answered. "I've come to offer a sacrifice to the LORD. Get yourselves ready to take part in the sacrifice and come with me." Samuel also invited Jesse and his sons to come to the sacrifice, and he got them ready to take part.

Samuel was God's _ r o _ _ _ t.

Saul was _ i _ g of Israel. Saul disobeyed God and was a b _ _ king.

Special o _ _ used to be poured on the _ e a _ of someone chosen to be a prophet, priest or king.

Do you ever think that when you're sad and sorry or angry because something isn't right, God might feel the same way?

Samuel was sad about Saul. So was God. Work out what God told Samuel:

Prayer: *Thank you God that you know everything and care when things aren't right. Please help me to trust you and be brave enough to do what you want, even when I'm scared.*

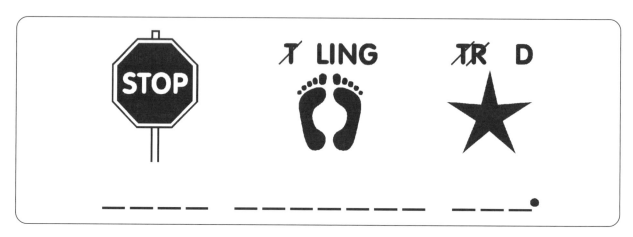

Missing words from previous page: prophet, king, bad, oil, head

48 God looks at the inside

Read 1 Samuel 16:6-12

⁶ When Jesse and his sons arrived, Samuel noticed Jesse's oldest son, Eliab. "He has to be the one the LORD has chosen," Samuel said to himself.

⁷ But the LORD told him, "Samuel, don't think Eliab is the one just because he's tall and handsome. He isn't the one I've chosen. People judge others by what they look like, but I judge people by what is in their hearts."

⁸ Jesse told his son Abinadab to go over to Samuel, but Samuel said, "No, the LORD hasn't chosen him." ...

¹⁰ Jesse had all seven of his sons go over to Samuel. Finally, Samuel said, "Jesse, the LORD hasn't chosen any of these young men. ¹¹ Do you have any more sons?"

"Yes," Jesse answered. "My youngest son David is out taking care of the sheep."

"Send for him!" Samuel said. "We won't start the ceremony until he gets here."

¹² Jesse sent for David. He was a healthy, good-looking boy with a sparkle in his eyes. As soon as David came, the LORD told Samuel, "He's the one! Get up and pour the olive oil on his head."

How do you usually judge people?

☐ They're good looking?
☐ They're rich?
☐ They're clever?
☐ They've lots of friends?

How can he be such a good player? He's so short!

You can't always judge a basketball player by his height!

God doesn't judge people like that. He sees what we're really like inside. He looks for people who try to please him.

Prayer: Lord God, I know I'm not really bad, but I'm not usually as good as I want to be either. I'm glad that you know I love you even when it doesn't look like it. Please keep my heart true to you.

49 Working for the king

'Hotshots, what can we do to cheer up old Mr Mangle who lives next to the church?'
'We could visit him and take him something nice to eat,' suggested Anna
'He could use some help to weed his garden,' said Chris.
'I know! A concert! Other lonely people might come too. We could sing songs and have a quiz and act out a play.'
'What a great idea!' said Jeff. 'Let's start planning.'

'David was a real star. He shone for God and made things brighter for others, even the king!' Saul was frightened so his officials wanted to cheer him up. Who do you know who needs some cheering up? How can you help them feel better? Ask God and other people for ideas.

Read 1 Samuel 16:16-18 & 22

16 "Your Majesty, let us go and look for someone who is good at playing the harp. He can play for you whenever the evil spirit from God bothers you, and you'll feel better."

17 "All right," Saul answered. "Find me someone who is good at playing the harp and bring him here."

18 "A man named Jesse who lives in Bethlehem has a son who can play the harp," one official said. "He's a brave warrior, he's good-looking, he can speak well, and the LORD is with him."

22 Not long after this, Saul sent another message to Jesse: "I really like David. Please let him stay with me."

Prayer:
Dear God, please help me to be like a shining light for you so that people feel brighter and happier when I'm around.

An unusual contest

Imagine turning up for a game on a hot day and the referee says, 'I have an idea. Instead of you all playing and getting hot and tired, why doesn't each team choose a representative and the two reps can play? Then whoever wins, we'll count that as a win for their team.'

Wars used to be fought this way between God's people and the Philistines. But why didn't anyone from Israel's army volunteer to fight the Philistine army's representative? *(See puzzle on page 75.)*

Read 1 Samuel 17:4-11

[4] The Philistine army had a hero named Goliath who was from the town of Gath and was nearly 3 metres tall. [5-6] He wore a bronze helmet and had bronze armour to protect his chest and legs. The chest armour alone weighed about 57 kilograms. He carried a bronze sword strapped on his back, [7] and his spear was so big that the iron spearhead alone weighed more than 7 kilograms. A soldier always walked in front of Goliath to carry his shield.

[8] Goliath went out and shouted to the army of Israel:

"Why are you lining up for battle? I'm the best soldier in our army, and all of you are in Saul's army. Choose your best soldier to come out and fight me! [9] If he can kill me, our people will be your slaves. But if I kill him, your people will be our slaves. [10] Here and now I challenge Israel's whole army! Choose someone to fight me!"

[11] Saul and his men heard what Goliath said, but they were so frightened of Goliath that they couldn't do a thing.

51 In the army

King Saul's army had no uniforms. They took their own weapons. Their families or friends brought them food. Today's armies are different.

Read 1 Samuel 17:14-19

¹⁴ David was Jesse's youngest son. ¹⁵ He took care of his father's sheep, and he went back and forth between Bethlehem and Saul's camp.

¹⁶ Goliath came out and gave his challenge every morning and every evening for 40 days.

¹⁷ One day, Jesse told David, "Hurry and take this sack of roasted grain and these ten loaves of bread to your brothers at the army camp. ¹⁸ And here are ten large chunks of cheese to take to their commanding officer. Find out how your brothers are doing and bring back something that shows that they're all right. ¹⁹ They're with Saul's army, fighting the Philistines in Elah Valley."

What did David take care of? ☐ ☐ ☐ ☐ ☐

How many brothers did David have? ☐ *(See page 71)*

How many brothers were younger than David? ☐

How many brothers joined the army? ☐

Every day Goliath came out to challenge Saul's army to send someone to fight him. No one dared.

How many times did Goliath shout out the challenge? (CLUE verse 16) ☐

Saul's army was scared of the Philistine enemy. They forgot they were God's people and that God could help them. Do bullies like Goliath make you scared? Well enjoy the rest of the story. There is Someone who sends bullies running!

Prayer idea:
There is fighting and war in so many countries around the world. Pray for people who live in scary situations and ask God to help them to trust him.

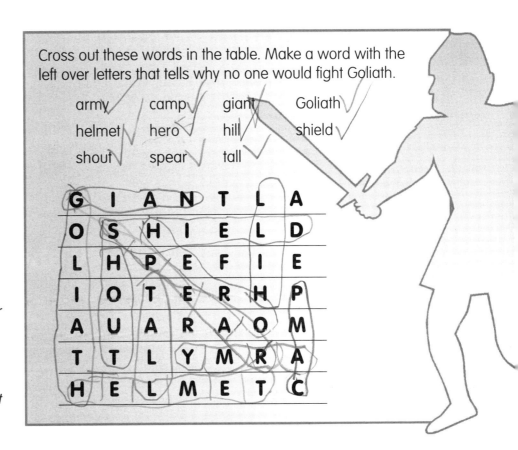

Cross out these words in the table. Make a word with the left over letters that tells why no one would fight Goliath.

army camp giant Goliath
helmet hero hill shield
shout spear tall

G	I	A	N	T	L	A
O	S	H	I	E	L	D
L	H	P	E	F	I	E
I	O	T	E	R	H	P
A	U	A	R	A	O	M
T	T	L	Y	M	R	A
H	E	L	M	E	T	C

52 On God's side

Read 1 Samuel 17:20-27

²⁰ David obeyed his father. He got up early the next morning and left someone else in charge of the sheep; then he loaded the supplies and started off. He reached the army camp just as the soldiers were taking their places and shouting the battle cry.
²¹ The army of Israel and the Philistine army stood there facing each other.
²² David left his things with the man in charge of supplies and ran up to the battle line to ask his brothers if they were well.
²³ While David was talking with them, Goliath came out from the line of Philistines and started boasting as usual. David heard him.
²⁴ When the Israelite soldiers saw Goliath, they were scared and ran off. ²⁵ They said to each other, "Look how he keeps coming out to insult us. The king is offering a big reward to the man who kills Goliath. That man will even get to marry the king's daughter, and no one in his family will ever have to pay taxes again."
²⁶ David asked some soldiers standing nearby, "What will a man get for killing this Philistine and stopping him from insulting our people? Who does that worthless Philistine think he is? He's making fun of the army of the living God!"
²⁷ The soldiers told David what the king would give the man who killed Goliath.

Sometimes people make fun of those who love God. This makes it tough, sometimes embarrassing, but God can help us stand up for him when that happens.

God's people were scared of the Philistines, especially Goliath, who were bullying them.

What did they need to remember?

G O W O U D H E P T H E M
 O   U L   E L   H

___ _____ ____ ____

Prayer: God, please help me to know that you are real and powerful even when others say that you are not. Give me the courage to let others know I belong to you.

53 Little things count

Although it was only a very small stone, Anna sure noticed it. Little things can make a big difference.

What very small part in each of these makes a big difference?

Read 1 Samuel 17:31-37

³¹ Some soldiers overheard David talking, so they told Saul what David had said. Saul sent for David, and David came. ³² "Your Majesty," he said, "this Philistine shouldn't turn us into cowards. I'll go out and fight him myself!"

³³ "You don't have a chance against him," Saul replied. "You're only a boy, and he's been a soldier all his life."

³⁴ But David told him:

"Your Majesty, I take care of my father's sheep. And when one of them is dragged off by a lion or a bear, ³⁵ I go after it and beat the wild animal until it lets the sheep go. If the wild animal turns and attacks me, I grab it by the throat and kill it."

Continued overpage

Little things count (continued ...)

1 Samuel 17:36-39

36 "Sir, I have killed lions and bears that way, and I can kill this worthless Philistine. He shouldn't have made fun of the army of the living God! 37 The LORD has rescued me from the claws of lions and bears, and he will keep me safe from the hands of this Philistine."

"All right," Saul answered, "go ahead and fight him. And I hope the LORD will help you."

38 Saul had his own military clothes and armour put on David, and he gave David a bronze helmet to wear. 39 David strapped on a sword and tried to walk around, but he was not used to wearing those things.

"I can't move with all this stuff on," David said. "I'm just not used to it."

David was tiny compared to Goliath but David knew God could protect him. He'd done it before.

Prayer: *Father God, sometimes I feel like I'm too small to make a difference. Please help me to be sure that with you I can do great things.*

54 God made 9 year olds!

'If only we knew as much as Jeff about basketball.'

'If only we could slam dunk like him!'

'I'd settle for being as tall as he is!'

'There's plenty of time for that. Be the best 9 year olds you can, team. God thinks 9 year olds are great. He doesn't want you to be grown up yet.'

King Saul lent David his armour to try to make him look like a big tough grown-up. It didn't work. David had to be himself. We all do, big or small.

Read 1 Samuel 17: 39-44

39 David took off the armour 40 and picked up his shepherd's stick. He went out to a stream and picked up five smooth stones and put them in his leather bag. Then with his sling in his hand, he went straight toward Goliath.

41 Goliath came toward David, walking behind the soldier who was carrying his shield. 42 When Goliath saw that David was just a healthy, good-looking boy, he made fun of him. 43 "Do you think I'm a dog?" Goliath asked. "Is that why you've come after me with a stick?" He cursed David in the name of the Philistine gods 44 and shouted, "Come on! When I'm finished with you, I'll feed you to the birds and wild animals!"

What weapons did David have?

_____

_____

Prayer: I sometimes wish I was bigger or older or had more things. Please help me to be confident enough to just be myself, God.

In the name of the Lord

'We could do a play about David and Goliath for Mr Mangle. Let's make Jeff Goliath!'

'I don't think so Dan. I know the end of this story.'

'Then tell us.'

'Let's read it together. I don't want to leave out any of the gory bits.'

Read 1 Samuel 17:45-51

⁴⁵ David answered:

"You've come out to fight me with a sword and a spear and a dagger. But I've come out to fight you in the name of the Lord All-Powerful. He is the God of Israel's army, and you have insulted him too!

⁴⁶ Today the Lord will help me defeat you. I'll knock you down and cut off your head, and I'll feed the bodies of the other Philistine soldiers to the birds and wild animals. Then the whole world will know that Israel has a real God.

⁴⁷ Everybody here will see that the Lord doesn't need swords or spears to save his people. The Lord always wins his battles, and he will help us defeat you."

⁴⁸ When Goliath started forward, David ran toward him. ⁴⁹ He put a stone in his sling and swung the sling around by its straps. When he let go of

Read 1 Samuel 17:45-51

one strap, the stone flew out and hit Goliath on the forehead. It cracked his skull, and he fell face down on the ground. ⁵⁰ David defeated Goliath with a sling and a stone. He killed him without even using a sword.

⁵¹ David ran over and pulled out Goliath's sword. Then he used it to cut off Goliath's head.

When the Philistines saw what had happened to their hero, they started running away.

Decode the message to see what David said to Goliath.

a = ✜   e = ✪   o = ♥   i = ✓

Y♥u h✜v✪ ✓nsult✪d G♥d. I h✜v✪ c♥m✪ t♥ f✓ght f♥r h✓m. Th✪ L♥rd w✓ll h✪lp m✪ d✪f✪✜t y♥u.

___ ____ _____ ___.
_ ____ ____ __ _____
___ ____. ___ ____ ____
____ __ _____ ___.

David wasn't fighting for himself; he was standing up for God. He wanted to show everyone that God is real – you can't keep insulting God expecting to get away with it.

God could have got rid of Goliath with a zap of lightning but he didn't. God often asks *people* to do things for him and there are things he wants *you* to do for him too. He may not ask you to kill a giant… But who knows?

God always gives us enough faith to do what he wants us to do.

Prayer idea:
Why don't you ask God what he would like you to do for him? Watch out for his answer and be ready to do it.

David's Crossword

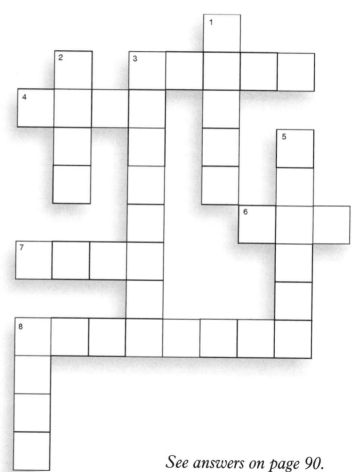

ACROSS

3. One of David's weapons
4. Where Goliath came from.
6. David was fighting for _____.
7. How many stones did David take?
8. People in the army.

DOWN

1. Huge person.
2. Goliath was very _____.
3. Looks after sheep.
5. David took 5 of these.
8. King _____.

See answers on page 90.

Sending letters in Bible times

Do you like getting letters? Usually the sender puts their letter in an envelope, buys a stamp and sends the letter through the post. Hey presto it turns up at your house!

In Bible times not everyone could write and there was no post. If you wanted to send a letter you gave it to a messenger to carry. There were no envelopes – you might even have to make your own paper, ink and pen.

HOW TO MAKE PAPER

1. Cut down papyrus reeds – they grow by the river.
2. Lay the stems across each other.
3. Beat them flat.
4. Dry them in the sun.
5. Rub them hard with a piece of bone or shell until smooth.

HOW TO MAKE INK

1. Take some soot from the fire.
2. Collect resin from a tree.
3. Mix them together with some olive oil.

Sending letters in Bible times

HOW TO MAKE A PEN

1. Find a hollow reed and shape the end to a point.
2. Dip it in the ink as you write.

There are lots of letters in the Bible. [That is letters written from one person to another, not a, b, c's]

Look up the Table of Contents for the New Testament. Skip the first 5 New Testament books and the last one. All the books in between are letters.

How many are there? ☐

Many of these letters were written by Paul the Apostle. Some were written to whole churches, others to just one person. But they weren't written just for them. They are also for us. They contain things that God wants us to know. In fact the whole Bible is like a huge letter from God to us.

Now we skip 1000 years of history to the time after Jesus returned to heaven leaving his friends to tell others about him. Meet a young friend called Timothy. There are two letters to him in our Bible, both were written by the apostle Paul.

Pass it on

'I've brought an old photo of me with my family,' said Jeff. The Hotshots gathered round.

'You were short then!' exclaimed Sam.

'Is that your Dad?' asked Anna. 'He's tall.'

'That's him. Notice I've got freckles like him too.'

'I've got a funny toe like my Dad,' said Dan. 'So has Grandma. Dad says funny toes run in our family.'

People in Timothy's family shared something special – Timothy, his mother and grandmother.

Read 2 Timothy 1:1-6

[1] From Paul, an apostle of Christ Jesus.

God himself chose me to be an apostle, and he gave me the promised life that Jesus Christ makes possible.

[2] Timothy, you are like a dear child to me. I pray that God our Father and our Lord Christ Jesus will be kind and merciful to you and will bless you with peace!

[3] Night and day I mention you in my prayers. I am always grateful for you, as I pray to the God my ancestors and I have served with a clear conscience. [4] I remember how you cried, and I want to see you, because that will make me truly happy. [5] I also remember the genuine faith of your mother Eunice. Your grandmother Lois had the same sort of faith, and I am sure that you have it as well. [6] So I ask you to make full use of the gift that God gave you when I placed my hands on you. Use it well.

Pass it on (continued ...)

What was the gift Paul gave Timothy?

Check your answer by colouring the shapes with a dot.

The love we have from God is not passed on through families in the same way as blue eyes or freckles. Families often share their faith and teach each other – as happened in Timothy's family. Of course everyone who loves God belongs to Jesus' family.

Who talks with you about loving God?

If you would like to be a part of God's family, see page 95.

Prayer idea: *Give thanks for anyone who has taught you about God. Remember relatives, people at church, even the people who make the Hotshots books.*

Lystra, where Timothy lived

Lystra was never as big or important as Jerusalem or even some of the big cities in Egypt, but its people were proud to live there. The Romans who ruled it thought it was important and even let the town make its own coins. Most Roman towns weren't allowed to do that.

Near the entrance to the town was a temple to Zeus, their chief god. People believed in lots of gods who thought they would help them if they sacrificed animals to them. The priest killed bulls at the temple to try and keep the gods happy. Worshippers gave offerings of flowers to the temple as well.

The priest wasn't right about Zeus or the other gods. The Bible says there is only one true God who made everything and Jesus is his son.

Paul believed that. He told Timothy and Timothy believed too.

After that Timothy didn't worship Zeus or sacrifice animals to him. He left Lystra and travelled to other towns to tell the people there about the one true God.

57 God at work

I wish we could see God

'You can see what he does,' Jeff told her. 'When people who love God do good things, that's God at work. Perhaps Timothy saw God heal a crippled man when Paul came to his town.'

Read Acts 14:8-11

[8] In Lystra there was a man who had been born with crippled feet and had never been able to walk. [9] The man was listening to Paul speak, when Paul saw that he had faith in Jesus and could be healed. So he looked straight at the man [10] and shouted, "Stand up!" The man jumped up and started walking around.

[11] When the crowd saw what Paul had done, they yelled out in the language of Lycaonia, "The gods have turned into humans and have come down to us!"

The crowds knew that only God could do what Paul did. So they thought he was God. They didn't know this secret.

GOD USES PEOPLE TO DO HIS WORK

Prayer: Lord God, It's amazing that you let ordinary people do the things you do. Help me to notice what you do through people.

58 God did it

'Last night I dreamed the Hotshots won the Grand Final. We played brilliantly and scored 100. Everyone cheered. They wanted to give us trophies, interview us for TV, get our autographs and give us sponsorships. It was awesome!'

Read Acts 14:14-15

14 When the two apostles found out about this, they tore their clothes in horror and ran to the crowd, shouting:

15 "Why are you doing this? We are humans just like you. Please give up all this foolishness. Turn to the living God, who made the sky, the earth, the sea, and everything in them."

Prayer: Father God, help people to know that when I do things for you, it's really you doing it, not me. Help me to become a person you can trust to work for you.

What did Paul tell the crowds? Tick two.

☐ I deserve all this praise.
☐ We're just ordinary people.
☐ Turn to the living God
☐ God's lucky to have me on his team.

If you'd been Timothy and saw what happened and heard Paul talk about God, what would you think?

Paul and Barnabas were beaten up and thrown out of town soon after they spoke. They came back much later and a church had started there!

59 Invisible but real

'Sorry I'm late, team.' Jeff rode up looking hot and tired, hair all over the place. 'That wind is really strong when you're riding against it.'

'I know,' said Chris. 'It's funny how something you can't even see can make such a huge difference.'

There's only one verse to read today:

Read 2 Timothy 1:7

⁷ God's Spirit doesn't want to make cowards out of us. The Spirit gives us power, love, and self-control.

We can't see God's Spirit, but he can make a huge difference in our life.

What does the Spirit give us?

_____, _____, _____

What doesn't he do?

_____

Answers to crossword on page 82.
Across: 3. Sling; 4. Gath; 6. God; 7. Five; 8. Soldiers;
Down: 1. Giant; 2. Tall; 3. Shepherd; 5. Stones; 8 Saul

'I don't understand!' said Anna. 'What's the Spirit?'

'Hard to understand, isn't it?' Jeff smiled, 'The Spirit is a person like God, in fact the Spirit is God. He's invisible and lives in us, helping us to live the way God wants.'

Is the Spirit in you?

Yes. And he's in everyone who loves God

Here are some of the other questions the Hotshots asked Jeff. Circle the correct answer.

Is the Spirit a good spirit? .... YES / NO

Is it the same as the Holy Spirit? .... YES / NO

Does the Spirit live in lots of people at once? ...... YES / NO

Is the Spirit in me? .... YES / NO

What am I?

I can show you what you are doing wrong.

I can train you to do good things.

I can make you wise.

I come from God.

Answer:

_____

_____

Invisible but real (continued ...)

EXTRA: If you want to know what the Spirit can do for you ...

Read Galatians 5:22-23

²² God's Spirit makes us loving, happy, peaceful, patient, kind, good, faithful, ²³ gentle, and self-controlled. There is no law against behaving in any of these ways.

Prayer:
Lord God thank you that you give your Spirit to everyone who loves you.

The Bible

'Why do we have the Bible at Hotshots?' asked Chris.

'Because Jeff thinks the Bible's the best, don't you Jeff?' said Anna quickly.

'I like other books too but the Bible is different. It tells us what God wants us to know.'

'And God wrote it, didn't he?' asked Emily.

'Yes and no,' Jeff answered. 'He didn't exactly write it himself, but he helped others to write it.'

'Do you mean he told them what to write?'

'That's right. I think that makes it worth reading. So let's do it!'

Read 2 Timothy 3:14-17

[14] Keep on being faithful to what you were taught and to what you believed. After all, you know who taught you these things. [15] Since childhood, you have known the Holy Scriptures that are able to make you wise enough to have faith in Christ Jesus and be saved. [16] Everything in the Scriptures is God's Word. All of it is useful for teaching and helping people and for correcting them and showing them how to live. [17] The Scriptures train God's servants to do all kinds of good deeds.

Do you know that millions of people all around the world read the Bible? Many will be reading it right now. Some might even be reading the same verses you've just read, perhaps in another language.

Who am I?

1. I was my father's favourite
   When I was a teenager I went to another country
   I was thrown into prison
   I saved my whole family _____

2. There was a temple in my town
   Paul wrote to me
   I lived in Lystra _____
   My mother and grandmother were Christians

3. I lived in Jerusalem
   I was always at the temple
   When I was 84
       I saw the Lord
   I was a prophet

4. I lived in Egypt
   My mother had a baby boy
   I talked to a real princess
   I watched a basket on the river

_____

**Check your answers from the Bible:
Genesis 37:3, 2 Timothy 1:5, Luke 2:36, Exodus 2:4
(Numbers 26:59).**

Three steps to a wonderful adventure

Thank you

Step One — Say thank you to God for loving you and for his promise to forgive you. Thank him for Jesus who came to show us the way and how to get rid of our sin.

Sorry

Step Two — Tell God you are sorry for the sin and wrong in your life. Ask him to forgive you.

How to be part of God's family.

When you decide to be a member of God's family, it is just like becoming Jesus' brother or sister!

Some people say yes, some say no.

There are three steps to begin.

Please

Step Three — Ask God to give you a new beginning and help you join his family. Ask him for his help to do what he says. Say a prayer like this in your own words. Write it on a piece of paper.

If you really mean what you say, you can be sure God hears you and that you're now part of his family.

Write the date you prayed this prayer:

_____

Certificate

Scripture Union
and
The Hotshots Team

This is to certify that

_____

[write your name neatly]

has completed the stories and projects from **Hotshots – Mini-stars of the Bible**

Signed: ......*Jeff*.. Jeff   (Hotshots Coach)

Countersigned: .... (Parent or other adult)

Date: ....